Ruminating
(verb) think deeply about something

Quinton A. Clawson

Copyright © 2017 Quinton A. Clawson
All rights reserved.
ISBN: 069256022X
ISBN-13: 978-0692560228

DEDICATION

To my beautiful, intelligent, and supportive wife, Daniela.
Without you, life would have no meaning.

And to my tenacious and resilient mother,
who sacrificed so much so that I could live.

ABOUT THE AUTHOR

    I attempted to write this section multiple times from the perspective of a professional publisher, but speaking about myself in the third person seems pretentious, so I've reserved myself to a more pragmatic approach.

    I was born in Honolulu, HI, and moved from state to state most my life. I began writing at the age of ten, but only began refining my work in my teenage years. Writing was always first and foremost a coping mechanism. It was a way of dealing with the abuse and abandonment of a father, and a way to express the struggles of a teenager growing up in a low socioeconomic household. It's fitting that my first publication will be a poetry collection, as poetry is where it all began.

    I spent my teenage years in Centreville, VA, and finished my Associates of Science in General Studies at Northern Virginia Community College. It was around this time that I began to write short stories, and began to play with the idea of writing a full-length book. I moved to Cape Coral, FL, and eventually received by Bachelors of Science in Psychology from Chaminade University. It was in my last year of undergraduate studies that I met Daniela.

    Daniela became the meaning in my life. She inspired me to complete my first book, which is yet published, and to pursue a graduate degree from the University of the Cumberlands in Professional Counseling. She gave me the confidence to begin this self-publication, to explore my career possibilities, and to continue writing. She is responsible for everything good in my life. We married on October 29th, 2016.

    Daniela and I still live in Cape Coral, FL with our two dogs, cat, umbrella cockatoo, and large assortment of arachnids and reptiles. I hope that after I complete my Masters, I will be in a position to pursue a PhD. in Clinical Psychology. I also hope to one day complete, and then publish, one of the many books I am working on.

    Thank you for taking the time to read my work. It is fulfilling to have the opportunity to share my thoughts, feelings, and life with you. I would love to connect with you, the reader, so please feel free to reach out to me through my social media below.

Instagram: @quintonaclawson
Twitter: @quintonclawson

CONTENTS

Introduction	1
Ruminating	3
LOVE	7
Getting Rid of Love	9
Beyond the Window	15
Her Name is Pendulum	17
And No One	19
My Pleasance	21
For Now, and Forever More	23
MORTALITY	25
Such is Life	27
The Spider and the Fly	29
Reckless	31
Tired	35
Passing into Haze	37
The Cartography of Life	39
SOCIETY	41
I Bet	43
Mankind	45
The Wild Mind	47
Fickle	49
I Caught a Raven	51
Where I Belong	53
I'm of a Dying Breed	55
The Young Man and the Monster	57
The Hype Before the Fall	59
When We Choose to Lie	61

CONTENTS

FAMILY	63
Staring Out the Kitchen Window	65
The Fruit Doesn't Fall Far	67
Abuse	69
Once in Fort Carson	71
Welcome to Our Future	73
My Foreboding Fraught	77
RELIGION	79
He Stood Upon the Pulpit	81
The Mirror	83
Don't Tell Me It's Not Cereal	85
I Wondered Upon a Star	87
And Wouldn't You Know?	89
You Don't Matter	91
POLITICS	93
An Innocent Man's Execution	95
What Meets the Eye	97
What a Great Turnout	99
White Castle	101
Black Lives Matter	103
So Little Left to Say	105
SHORT STORIES	107
Leave a Light On	109
Until Death Do Us Part	113
Through the Window	115
That Taxi Ride	117
The Bee	121
NOTHING REALLY ENDS	123

INTRODUCTION

    I have always been plagued by the curse of overthinking, and though I can admit some benefits to this sickness, it most often results in a chaotic web of tangents that never result in a conclusion.

    It was on one such occasion of overthinking that I wrote the poem that shares the title of this collection, Ruminating. This poem was an experiment. It was an attempt to resist the urge to filter the many ideas bouncing around within my head. I started by simply writing about the first thing I thought of, and when that thought had passed, writing about the next. The result was a piece of poetry that any outsider might refer to as lunacy, but which I valued more than any poem I had previously written.

    I never wrote the poem, Ruminating, with the intention of it being the beginning to a poetry collection, but alas, here we are. So after coming to the conclusion that this poem would be the spearhead for my first publication, I began to piece together how I would organize the rest. Ruminating seems to jump from one topic to the next, and so I summed up these topics as best I could into six categories. I then focused on finding other pieces of poetry that I had written that would fit within each category, and with these, I parted this collection into sections. Do not be fooled though. This collection of poems is not meant to be represented chronologically and organized, but meant to be represented in the way that I view the reality of life, chaotic.

    I've found that in this chaotic life, answers are only ever subjective and temporary, whereas questions are universal and immortal. So, although you may infer meaning from the words I use to express thoughts throughout this collection, know that I would never intend to offer answers, but that I'm only ruminating.

Quinton A. Clawson

Ruminating

She made the world jealous with the stars in her eyes,
and fluttered her eyelashes how the hummingbird flies.
Enchantingly breathtaking...

She had suffocated more than one boy,
with the toy,
of her coy,
she would employ.
And her flickering tongue lavishly brought joy,
while her quips quickly quelled and sought to destroy.
And the many fools of the day,
enjoyed to say,
that once, oh yes once,
this monster asked them to stay.
They would FUCK,
and they would fight,
and all in one night,
they'd put out the lights,
of a sky gone gray.

In the celebration of existentialism,
I suppose this looked fine,
though it seems to me that she was a nihilist,
not in her right mind.
But my criticisms don't change the sound of a song,
and logical behavior doesn't make a psychopath wrong.
So what does it matter?

In trench coats they waited for a lull in the boredom of their lives,
and in rain,
so I've heard,
witches just want to stay dry.
So of course in a barrel like that,
you can do little more than try,
but were not apples,
but oranges,
and peaches,
and figs,
and the world's not that simple,
but we put it in a barrel...

Quinton A. Clawson

And I try to be fair,
because my judgements don't change the perception of an artist,
and sometimes being quiet is how you get the farthest.
So I pick up a pen filled with the ink of the dreams of the failures,
and I make a few of my own.

The good news for that slut,
is that eventually everything ends,
that is,
when we die.
And if you've heard the good news,
than I'm sure you've heard too,
that we're all sinners.
So what do we do?
And if Satan is such a bad guy,
than can you please tell me why,
he punishes the lie,
and the lust,
and the gluttony,
and the greed,
and the vanity,
and the wrath,
and the pride
and the sloth,
and the sin.
Wouldn't that make him an angel?
And if so, who's God?

I'm still not satisfied,
answers are nothing more than preludes to another question,
and I guess that's a good thing,
but I'm as satisfied as starvation,
like the people we refuse to help,
because we're all too important for them to be cared about,
too busy to talk about the effects of a drought,
to stand and to shout,
to argue and to spout,
and we're too busy with nationalism,
to be humans.

She's dead now…
Her makeup smeared like a hooker's last night.
She may have had it coming,

Ruminating

but she never asked for it.
So I'm asking questions to dead people,
like do you believe in fate?
How about love?
I can't contemplate,
what resides above.
Nothing I debate,
until push comes to shove.
You see,
we're all demons.
I suffocate,
like a hand in a glove,
trying to resuscitate,
this little white dove,
while I wait,
for what's already done.

She's dead,
and I'm ruminating.

Quinton A. Clawson

LOVE

Love is a confounding thing.
In a rational sense, it is simply a chemical reaction, the amygdala
flooding the body with endorphins and other neurochemicals; an
evolutionary adaptation to further the species.
In an irrational sense, it is the mysterious bond of two humans, which
leads them to a utopian harmony, or grips them long after they've torn
each other apart.

Quinton A. Clawson

Getting Rid of Love

I stood upon the patio,
and knocked upon the door,
waiting for an answer,
for which I was called for.

They call me a doctor,
I heal and mend like they do,
but a degree is that I lack,
though my results are still true.

A man he did come answer,
a pathetic looking slob,
hint of alcohol on his breath,
cheeks to befriend a sob.

"Hello," I exclaimed,
you called of this, that I'm sure,
I'm here to help you friend,
I've come bearing the cure.

He smiled in comprehension,
corners touching cheeks,
"come in, come in," he said,
I've been expecting you for weeks.

I peered into the doorway,
cautious step and then two,
the house was in disarray,
filth easily in view.

"Yes, I'm quite busy,"
and to this is what he replied,
"well where should we begin,"
as his composed smile lied.

I gave a pitied grin and said,
"first I would like some coffee,"
then from there we can begin,
shaking eyes off of me.

Quinton A. Clawson

I found his couch and moved the trash,
while he queried but didn't question,
I sat down and moved some vermin,
while he headed to the kitchen.

The empty bottles there laid stacked,
Upon the table in the room,
I simply nudged them from where they stood,
and made myself feel at home.

"Do you mind if I smoke," I said,
hearing drips into a mug,
"no please do, as I do" he said,
ashe stains throughout his rug.

He returned with my drink,
but none for him as I could see,
"sorry about the mess," he said,
as he sat across from me.

"I've seen worse," I offered,
adding some sugar and some cream,
he stared at me ever nervously,
held to bust at the seam.

I took a sip of the liquid,
it was a cheap bitter taste,
and although quite a busy man,
I had to keep from my haste.

After a few tense minutes,
and giving my cigarette a shove,
I asked him what he's been waiting for,
"so you want to get rid of love?"

"Yes!" he nearly shouted,
"I want to forget, I want no pain,
I want this wretched thing out of me,
I just can't remove this wicked stain."

Ruminating

"Remove the words within my ears,
the feel of her lips to that of mine,
the memories that we had shared,
my self-loathing trait of swine."

"I want to feel numbing grace,
delete these pictures from my head,
I don't want them, I don't want it,
I want to feel nothingness instead."

I listened intently to his requests,
eyes fixated to his cues,
remaining silent into silence,
until even more silence ensued.

He retracted his outburst,
from the uneasy lack of words,
I looked out the grimy window,
and passed, a couple songbirds.

"You can't help me can you?"
He inquired, and then he said,
"I knew it wasn't really true,
I'd much rather be dead."

I took another drag,
countering while I inhaled,
"what you heard is true," I said,
and his ghostly face paled.

"Yes I can make it stop,
I can take it all away,
but do you know the cost to you?
Are you prepared to pay?"

He looked hopefully fearful,
"I have no money, just a heart,
I interrupted him immediately,
money will not play the part.

"See here's the thing," I continued,
"I'm quite familiar with your curse,
there's a few things we'll have to do,
the cure will be short, and it will be terse.

First we'll remove your eyes,
cut them straight from their socket,
you'll never see her again,
her vision removed from the docket.

Then it's the ears,
useless contraptions at best,
we'll scoop out the drums too,
from her voice you'll have rest.

You did not yet mention,
but I should suggest,
removing your nose too,
would be for the best.

Smell is the strongest sense,
tied to bad memories,
so a whiff of her perfume,
could turn nightmares from dreams.

Now touch is a hassle,
so many nerves, so yes,
first we'll remove your hands,
then cauterize the rest.

Now this will be torture,
this will be nothing but pain,
but what could be more painful?
Then her as your bane.

Next is your mind,
you'll see her still without eyes,
so then I'll grab my pick
and we'll lobotomize.

Ruminating

I should take your tongue,
Yes, we'll remove that too,
God forbid you accidentally,
call her to you.

Lastly, but most important,
we'll have to remove the core,
so out will come your heart,
and then there's nothing more."

I completed the terms,
and he thought for a moment,
and then he nodded approval,
as such, his enrollment.

So I completed my work,
now he lives without pain,
not much of a man,
but alive, somewhat sane.

We all want to live,
so life, chose this cur,
but what is living really,
when living without her.

Quinton A. Clawson

Beyond the Window

I can hear her heart,
in the cold of halls,
and how cold it is,
for a day so bright.

Elegance does not define her,
grace doesn't do her justice,
as she effortlessly floats beyond the window,
in a simply extravagant fashion.

She contains more purpose,
than could ever be offered,
by someone with mortal means,
or a God of lustful fury.

She captivates,
she radiates,
she appears just as suddenly,
as she leaves.

And in a second's stupor,
the love that had conjured,
in a soulful place,
is torn.

You are but a whisper,
a gust of wind,
a reason to flip her hair,
an egotistical lesson.

And when the beating stops,
when the cold halls become colder,
the windows seem to darken,
and the air becomes thinner.

Quinton A. Clawson

Her Name is Pendulum

There is a pendulum in my mind,
and it swings life away,
back and forth spending time,
but you stand in its way.

And with a hand you do so grasp,
the ticking of the clock,
making every moment last,
the key unto my lock.

And the world says hurry up,
we have but seconds left,
but then you take my hand, my love,
and as one we take a breath.

I smell flowers and I see stars,
I hear the roar of the artist's brush,
I wave to all the passing cars,
no longer in a rush.

I smile, I laugh, I love,
in each heart I see a gleaming,
like a hand fit to a glove,
you give my life it's meaning.

Quinton A. Clawson

And No One

It took me years to find you,
years waiting to feel complete,
years feeling empty,
years attempting to find my reason
my purpose.

In an instant you offered me everything,
happiness,
love,
a future with meaning.

You offered me a haven where the past only matters,
because it's the story of how I met you.

My muse,
I feel days old,
I was dead before I met you.

You breathed life into my bones,
and gave them a heart to hold.

Without you,
I dare not say it,
because you and to be without,
makes me nonexistent.

I once thought vows were just words,
to deny our insecurities,
but now I know that vows,
are words that can't explain,
the love I feel for you,
my promise,
my prose.

You are my heart,
my purpose,
my life,
and I will only love,
have only loved,
you, only you,
and no one.

Quinton A. Clawson

My Pleasance

My hearts pressed against hers,
in this old lover's fashion,
I need not define,
this unexpected passion.

She smiles,
it radiates,
it lights my soul to a simmer.
I need nothing more,
than for her eyes to glimmer.

And as her hand slowly,
just caresses my palm,
I'm overwhelmed,
I'm captivated,
by this soothing calm.

She whispers so gently,
"don't leave me just yet,"
and it took but one week,
for years since we met.

Her lips they're divine,
her eyes are a dream,
and her dreams,
there they stir,
to the seams so it seems.

In photographs and paint,
this anxiety is reached,
the talent of talents,
here it is breached.

Her back there it bends,
into an insatiable arch,
her body,
my fingers,
loving her in the dark.

Quinton A. Clawson

She's the canvas of a painting,
the Mona Lisa of our time,
the David of the world,
the words to my rhyme.

My essence breathes her in,
her hair unravels in grace,
and its here,
here with her,
my safe haven, my place.

I trace her face with my fingertips,
and brush the hair that there pries,
she bites,
bites her lip,
and then closes her eyes.

To be the man that here holds her,
to just be blessed with her presence,
I would have never thought that here,
is where I'd find my pleasance.

For Now, and Forever More

What is a fireplace with no logs?
But a hole with no heat,
like a pie without a filling,
tastes all the less sweet.

And what is a vase without decoration,
but lacking of potential,
like a storm without rain,
is far from torrential.

Like the black sky without stars,
or the blue sky without clouds,
they are a void, a hollow,
like a mall without crowds.

A box of chocolates is just a box,
when the candies are devoured,
and a car is just its metals,
without an engine to be powered.

And I am just a husk,
an animated corpse at best,
without the love of your heart,
buried deep within my chest.

I'm a pond without water,
just a ditch with some weeds
or the waterfall with no fall,
or the farmer with no seeds.

You're the arrow in my compass,
guiding my heart safely through,
you're the wick to my wax,
there's no light without you.

You're the purpose and the reason,
you're the love of my heart's core,
you're the blood that makes it beat,
for now, and forever more.

Quinton A. Clawson

MORTALITY

Death comes for us all.
I find it perplexing that humans have spent so much time and effort concerning themselves with the concept of mortality, or better yet, how to avoid being subject to it.
The truth is, we are but specks on an infinite timeline, and our lives matter little. That may seem disheartening, but I find that the meaning in my life comes from the idea that it has no meaning at all.

Quinton A. Clawson

Such is Life

First, we are simply an idea,
nestled between two lovers,
our fates still undecided,
waiting for mistake or choice,
to carry us into existence.

Then we are nothing but naive,
wide-eyed and ignorant,
gaping at a mysterious world,
our understanding to be decided,
by those that remain closest.

Next, we are wonder and faith,
the world before a vision,
chased by theories of unrealism,
that we don't quite yet grasp,
but are all the more aware of.

Afterwards we are emotions,
full of inadequacy and justification,
seeking the undeniable truth,
of what we've seen and been told,
and what we know should be.

Following, we are life's frustrations,
realizing the reality of what we are,
but seeking something we aren't,
scrutinized by a mirror of inaptitude,
and shadowed by our uncertainty.

After that we are stagnant appreciation,
accepting life's choices and placement,
placing what we never were in children,
and displacing our subconscious anger,
on the peers that feel just the same.

Now we are age and experience,
no longer concerned with what will be, but what is sure to come,
we analyze the life we've led,
the choices we've made,
and realize that it was all for naught.

Quinton A. Clawson

Last, we are just a simple memory,
appreciated in a superficial sense,
a gravestone, or ash on water,
allowing a passing to come forth,
to allow another life to begin.

The Spider and the Fly

A fly slowly drifted,
clumsily on wind,
until he was snared,
by a web oh so thin.

The fly was aware,
that his fate had been sealed,
but he fought oh he wrestled,
until his wings had been peeled.

Struggling and close,
to freedom at last.
The spider that dwelled,
approached oh so fast.

The fly having realized,
that his cause was for naught,
stopped tugging and pulling,
and laid limp in his spot.

"I am here my small dinner,
I won't make you wait,"
said the spider prepared,
to make a tense plate.

The fly did not plead.
He only sat their staring,
watching his reaper drool,
and calmly preparing.

"You do not scream,
and you do not yell,
you're unique that's for sure
but why? Do tell."

The fly then responded,
as a philosopher does,
with just one word,
one word, "Because."

Quinton A. Clawson

The spider he stared,
just oh so confused,
his stomach rumbling,
his ego bruised.

And that stomach did call,
so his curiosity did dwindle.
He forgot the exchange,
and made use of his spindle.

While gorging himself,
on the corpse of the fly,
a bird just so happened,
to fly right on by.

Taking notice of the spider,
the bird doubled back,
to pursue his new interest,
the distracted snack.

Landing on a branch,
that held the thin web,
the bird did look down,
and the spider, in dread.

The spider did scream,
because he didn't understand,
what the fly had known,
that we all die in the end.

And so it continued,
like the fly, he was lost.
To the bird it was normal,
but to him it was chaos.

Reckless

Let us be reckless!
Life is not determined by fate,
but by choices,
and your choice,
bores me.

I cannot abide,
by what society deems,
a normal existence.
I will pay the bills,
but not without splurging,
and I will drive the car,
to the job,
that I refuse to hate,
and when they say,
"in a few years,"
I will say,
"no."

I shall be reckless.

I will quit and pursue,
the next best thing,
until that becomes the worst,
and when my checking account,
subtracts to zero,
I shall spend,
five more dollars.
I shall smoke,
and drink,
and enjoy every vice,
that this world has to offer.
Critics will argue,
live fast,
die young,
and I will respond,
that my recklessness,
is not a loss,
but a gain,
for living isn't living,
if you're walking on egg shells,

and I'm neither careful,
nor frightened,
I'm reckless.

I will love without regret,
and never regret love,
and I will give her my all,
and if,
and when,
she shatters everything I've given,
I'll send her a message,
that will smile with repetition,
"I was not afraid to live,
nor afraid to love,
maybe a bit afraid of your choices,
but I'm reckless."

I will take every loan,
to achieve fulfillment,
and when I'm asked,
"how will you pay?"
I will answer,
"in time."
They'll gasp, and they'll mock.
Accountants will refer to me,
as a fool.
However, I will persevere,
with six classes in a semester,
an internship,
and a job,
they'll think they misjudged me,
when really,
I'm just reckless.

My family,
will be concerned,
and they'll weep on Thanksgiving,
when I don't arrive,
because I've made plans,
to travel,
a week before the date,
to some far off place,
that few have heard of.

They'll comment,
"I hope he gets it together soon.
His wife must be suffering too.
Isn't he just so reckless?"

I'll write poetry,
that won't rhyme,
and short stories,
that don't make sense,
and when I finish a novel,
my few fans will faint,
at the recklessness,
of the profanity,
with which I've flooded the pages.
They'll say I'm crazy,
and I'll say, "no,
you got it right,
the first time."

I'll die,
maybe young,
maybe old.
Maybe I stopped being reckless,
and regretted every day,
I paid my bills,
got in my car,
drove to the job,
that I hate,
for a promotion,
that will come,
in five years,
if I wait.

Quinton A. Clawson

Tired

I'm tired,
but I can't sleep,
like the moon that falls,
but is there when the sun rises,
or the child that screams,
because he knows when he stops,
when his tantrum has ceased,
his eyelids will close.

I'm as drowsy as the watchman,
making his midnight rounds,
or the barista,
hopped up,
on espresso grounds.
I'm the bats in the sky,
whom fly with the birds,
the light in the library,
with the student,
learning his words.

I'm tired,
and have yet to rest,
like the martyr with a purpose,
strapped to his chest,
I'm so very tired,
but I can't sleep,
awake with myself,
counting these sheep.

Quinton A. Clawson

Passing Into Haze

I feel myself drifting,
lazily I wander,
trapped within my head,
with words left to ponder.

It's irritably unquenchable,
this feeling that I have,
a disinterested illusion,
a hollow beaten path.

And when I dream at day,
I often have to ask,
do others notice me,
and my forgotten task.

Do they see my gaze,
looking past their face,
past their existence,
passing into haze.

Do they ask themselves,
where is he today?
Does he even listen?
Will he even stay?

This was just a stop,
a place to rest my head,
and I will travel on,
until I reach my bed.

Quinton A. Clawson

The Cartography of Life

The pendulum swings,
rhythmically back and forth,
the cartographers of life,
set their ships for due north.

The bow has a better view,
than what is seen from the nest,
but proves to be hazardous,
when met by a crest.

But wouldn't it be beautiful,
to see a world from a wave,
to meet your peak in seconds,
and in seconds meet your grave?

Wouldn't it be beautiful,
to let the wind sweep away,
everything you ever knew,
and bring a new day?

It would be beautiful,
to escape from the cabin,
to meet the ocean as is,
and see what would happen.

It would be beautiful,
to wake up when beached,
to stand upon the sand,
and see what you've reached.

Stand with the bow,
let the salt touch your face,
admire the horizon,
and feel the currents grace.

Because the hands of a clock,
spin despite where you stand,
so find the best spot,
and make it the best that you can.

Quinton A. Clawson

SOCIETY

Society is simply the result of humans living together in an organized fashion, and yet, it's come to mean so much more than that.
I believe in the individual, and as an individual, society is nothing but an annoyance. It represents what one must cope with to behave in a beneficial manner. It represents those people and beliefs that coincide with mine, and also those that do not.
It is that part of society that I lack congruence with that annoys me the most, and which has been much of the inspiration for the following works.

Quinton A. Clawson

I Bet

I bet I can find a whore at a party,
and a tool of a man feeding her shots.
A drug addict overdoses and dies,
because it's not cool to call the cops.

I bet I can find a frat boy at a college,
who has roofied a freshman or two,
and the ones that he didn't,
still slept with him,
because he said I love you.

I bet there's a man ignoring the cries,
of a child he knows is his son,
but he's just too conceited,
and he's just too selfish,
and most of all he's just too damn young.

I bet there's a mother that he left on her own,
who will struggle, who will fail, who will die,
and the son will repeat the cycle of his father,
because curses responded his cries.

I bet I would hear a hypocritical pastor,
who damns the sinners to hell,
because we can't just forgive,
and we can't just live,
we take religion, and fear, and we sell.

I bet I could find a man on political hill,
who claims he wants best for you and I,
so long as there are six zeros,
and an image to call a hero,
the government is easy to buy.

I bet I would smell the odor,
of the poor, the needy, the homeless,
and the ignorance of a public,
that would prefer to ignore this.

And I bet that the person,
who sits hungry and homeless,
was once the whore at a party,
and is still just looking for shots.

I bet I could find a lie on your breath,
and a deception on your face,
if I looked closely at all the signs,
and if I put the pieces in place.

Mankind

Meet mankind,
making marvelous,
massive mammoths,
muttering and musing,
it was mandatory.

After anxious action,
and aching absurdity,
an accustomed attitude,
against acknowledgement,
anchors attainment.

Never knowing need,
naturally nearing negligence,
not neat or normal,
nor nearly neutral,
begging nervousness.

Kickoff to the kindness,
that the king kills,
keeping kiosks of keys,
within an unkind keep,
that considers only kinfolk.

In insidious ignorance,
ignoring the itemized injured,
idolizing immoral ideals,
impatient and impulsive,
indicting incidents.

Nevertheless,
the next news,
is neither noisy nor naked,
not necessarily negative,
nailing needles in none.

Definitively destructive,
and delighting in dominance,
despite divisive demise,
I doubt the default design,
and defiantly determine we're demons.

Quinton A. Clawson

The Wild Mind

And here I am again,
in between the bars of a skull that's become a prison.
Oh, why do I even try?
When my mind becomes the monster that it is.
I think,
well I think it might just need some space.

I feed it biscuits,
hoping for a little understanding,
but oh it's a ferocious thing.
And you can't tame a wild beast,
so I'm running again,
as it rages on.

It's relentless,
it's as strong as I am weak,
and the worst part is,
it never wants to sleep,
but I coax it into hibernation,
and the silence is such a beautiful thing.

I lie down beside my sleeping thoughts,
and they stir and they crawl.
I hold them,
and for once,
I think we've found a balance,
a reason not to fight anymore.

You can't tame a wild beast though.
I know I knew better.
My mind bites the fingers that feed it,
and as I bleed,
it roars in success,
and I've grown impatient.

I become the monster now.
I swing and I fight.
I challenge the very thing I created,
but it's a clever mass of emotions,
it makes a hasty escape,
and I'm alone again.

Quinton A. Clawson

Here in this cage,
the one that is my mind,
I watch my ideas dance around me,
fully in view,
never in grasp,
until they return between the bars again.

They sweep their fingers through my hair,
and we dance together across the floor,
We hold each other closely,
as I coddle them like my daughters,
but you can't tame a wild beast,
and everything leaves.

Through the bars with you again,
they creep silently away.
I reach out for them,
"please don't leave me,"
hold my hand,
no… you can't tame a wild beast.

Fickle

Two oval sapphires stare intently at me,
and if it were that easy I'd make me their setting.
It's their call that I interpret to mean,
why won't you love me with your fickle being?

My virtue is a conscious uncertainty,
and I am not perfect for everything I am,
but to be perfect would be to be Godly,
and God is an imperfect man.

As I turn my back on the two ocean blue jewels,
I am overcome with a sense of loss,
thoughts flail flirtatiously about,
I want to strip my flesh and my flaws.

This heavy, burdening thick skin,
it's weight unbearable in these halls,
as I travel amongst my filthy fellows,
on all fours, and all paws.

Similar to a swarm of locusts,
or a clutch of freshly made maggots,
a brood of clustering clumsy cockroaches,
to appear, is to wreak havoc.

I reached a transparent door that wasn't so clear,
I listened to the creeping footsteps of my kin,
swathed in gaudy dressings of mating displays,
intent on arousing their sexual selection.

Of all the insects I've encountered,
and of all the beasts I've ever known,
we're not so distant, them and us,
I exited, and I went home.

I Caught a Raven

I caught a raven by its tail,
it fluttered, yet it did not flail,
and before it could up and fly away,
I slammed it inside a cage,

It didn't scream, yelp, or holler,
but accepted scene against desire,
shocked or calm I shall never know,
imprisoned though I was never foe.

I kept it there for what I deem as days,
there where I beam, and there it stays,
telling friends of the young captured soul,
never accepting the eventual toll.

Until a day the raven began to sing.
The beautiful soft song would ring,
Across empty halls,
        and abandoned rooms.
Amongst bitter aromas,
        and smoky fumes.

It stopped its song for just a moment,
bit the latch that would prolong it,
worked at it with its full avail,
until the cage was an empty shell.

So now here I sit once again,
remembering my long-gone friend,
waiting for the next raven to come my way,
to sit in this cage,
        where it shall stay.

Quinton A. Clawson

Where I Belong

The fire lights the tobacco of my pipe,
and it crackles its intent upon my demeanor,
the smoke laughs blissfully into my lungs,
a masochistic sensation I hold applause for.

Here is where I belong,
in this controversial wavering stance,
with a smoldering beverage,
that waits to enlighten,
or a chilled drink,
amidst icebergs,
that numbs.

More fire, more water,
more fingers passionately grazing keys,
more shameful attempts at comradery,
more vehement statements of artistry.
More! I want more!

But here is where I belong,
not with the ghosts of my attempts,
not with the fate that I scrawl on my heart,
in this moment, now,
here is where I belong.

Quinton A. Clawson

I'm of a Dying Breed

I've come to accept the fact,
that I am of a dying breed.
A group of men and women,
fading to obscurity.

Born in the same year,
that we should have died,
We live and we struggle,
because we have tried.

Superficial at best,
are the interests of this world,
we are ignored, we are silenced,
and then we are spurned.

I am a writer.
I am a species extinct.
I write because I am,
and I am because I speak.

I have so much to offer,
but my chances are bare.
How does a doctor heal patients,
if nobody's there?

We can evoke emotion,
we promote free speech.
We bring about change,
and we're a tool to teach.

We could catalyze world peace,
end the anger in men,
I thought that the sword,
was weaker than the pen.

But who likes a writer,
when nobody reads?
Because everything we read,
can be seen on TV.

But there's more to blame,
than a common distraction,
we stopped caring as people,
we stopped being human.

We wanted convenience,
so we found an easier pace,
we stopped using our words,
we stopped showing our face.

So my argument is,
that I'm of a dying breed,
not because I lost importance,
but because people lost need.

In a world where how we look,
means more than what we say,
In a world where our actions mean less,
every single day.

The Young Man and the Monster

There's a song of long ago,
that speaks of a young man,
who found himself in a struggle,
with a monster of the land.

The man was similar to all,
and stronger than none,
lacked the skill of a warrior,
intimidation of a gun.

But determined he was,
to see his task through,
he faced his demon,
as we all do.

In the morning they met,
conjured from his heart,
the beast appeared to him,
and the battle did start.

From his mind came minions,
who assisted the fiend,
the weak boy buckled,
and his spine leaned.

But to the boy's side,
came something unexpected,
the strength of his soul,
which the darkness was vexed with.

Despite the boy's weakness,
it seemed he could win,
but quite a struggle it was,
for him and only him.

The years passed slowly,
and in constant shifting,
of who was losing,
and who was winning.

Then something happened,
the boy was assisted,
by friends he met with,
and family that visited.

Strangers came too,
because it seemed only right,
how can one do nothing,
when suffering is in sight?

The demon and minions,
that he held in his fold,
couldn't bare the strength,
of more than one human soul.

The world came together,
humanity united as one,
fighting the evil they created,
led by a man that was young.

And as possible as it seems,
this is just a story to be read,
to entertain our children,
and keep our ignorance fed.

Because while we tell them at night,
the monsters are under the bed,
there are beasts living in our heart,
and demons within our head.

The Hype Before the Fall

I've spent the better part of my life,
listening to the squabbles of men and women,
over the opposites of necessity,
rhythmically aware that in their claims,
an ignorance brews.

Like a child whose left the toy store,
but still screams for a gift,
the war is lost,
but the battle's not over,
and we could die for better things.

However,
It's the spectator's wish,
to live within the drama,
opinion manifests popularity,
and we will kill to be known.

Because a name in a book is better,
than a life led in morality,
so instead of succumbing to thought,
we take the stage as right,
and forget we were wrong.

And it's in this moronic display,
humanity will crumble beneath its own weight,
like building a steeple for the world to see,
while disregarding the pillars beneath,
it's only pretty so long as they hold.

So now here we are,
architects empty of forethought,
and I have little faith we will plan,
before grasping for our tools.
The hype before the fall.

Quinton A. Clawson

When We Choose to Lie

In touch with intuition,
and intrinsic intentions,
is uninviting to investors,
and this is the cost…

Of a cynical blunt rationalism,
of an overwhelming honesty,
which is only worthy of acceptance,
but often met with anger.

To shy away from stating logical conclusions,
is to lie by omitting a statement,
and I'm neither a liar, nor a coward,
so I vehemently state facts.

But it's a lonely occasion,
one met with a crowd,
but ended with a podium,
filled with cognitive dissonance.

To cease, would be to surrender,
to accept truth as insignificant,
when emotions become tangible,
and we choose to lie.

Quinton A. Clawson

FAMILY

Family has always been a bit of an enigma to me. I have never understood those that force their close social bonds, such as those who choose to subject themselves to negative experiences during holidays for the sake of blood relations. I cannot take part in the tradition of faking smiles with those I dislike, and I have too often seen the habit slowly rot the happiness of many.

Quinton A. Clawson

Staring Out the Kitchen Window

They play baseball in backyards,
as ice cream rolls by,
screaming, "timeout,"
to spend their allowance,
on popsicles of dreams,
and hope flavored sprinkles.

We played guns in the streets,
fingers pointed outwards,
screaming, "bang, bang,"
until our friends would collapse,
never thinking that one day,
they might just be real.

They return after their games,
to houses of brick,
screaming, "I'm home,"
mothers cooking dinner,
fathers catching news,
taking baths before bed.

We returned after our nights,
to houses of straw,
whispering, "shh, shh,"
to the friend we brought home,
for a little bit of intimacy
and time spent alone.

And they stare in at us,
to futures untold,
screaming, "forward,"
with near new bicycles,
brand name clothes,
never knowing the word want.

And we stare out at them,
knowing we did well,
screaming, "thank you,"
to the parents we had,
the one's that we didn't,
and the one we are now.

Quinton A. Clawson

The Fruit Doesn't Fall Far

So it goes to show,
as you all should know,
the fruit doesn't fall far from the tree.
Unless you kick it about,
turn it inside and out,
and bruise it so all can see.

The fruit will adapt,
through it's right to react,
and the seeds will grow tougher than pits,
a new tree will be,
more than you or than me,
and it will grow from its merciless zone.

Then, in that ideal,
it will scar and then heal,
and it will challenge the needles you've tossed.
It will breed its own cones,
create its own home,
and in time, you'll be the one who is lost.

And when your trunk has been chopped,
from a stump it is lopped,
and your ground to the pulp you deserve,
your seed will still be,
taller than you or than me,
with many rings to tell of the lesson.

Quinton A. Clawson

Abuse

Hit her again,
that will teach her a lesson,
don't you step out of line,
is the theme of this session.

Be what I want,
and don't you dare change,
your mine to shape,
so your mind I'll rearrange.

Were you looking at him?
Because that's what I saw.
Well we'll just be safe,
and I'll break your jaw.

Baby I love you,
I'll never do it again,
I know I can change,
and I will until when…

I'm drunk, that's right,
who are you to judge me?
Why don't we add bruises,
where no one can see.

You fuck up everything,
and once again you burnt dinner?
Can you do anything right?
Could you get a bit thinner?

God you look fat.
You should probably eat less,
I won't dare be seen with you,
when you're looking a mess.

Tell them you fell,
it won't happen again, I swear,
I'll get some real help,
I can prove that I care.

Quinton A. Clawson

Yes, I've been going,
I meet with the group once a week,
now get off my back,
who are you to question me?

What do you mean someone called?
Oh, she's from the office,
no there's nothing going on,
why wouldn't I be honest?

What do you mean you found the messages?
Have you been going through my stuff?
Get over here you bitch,
I'll show you who's tough.

The doctors are suspicious.
What did they ask you?
I told you I was sorry.
You need to lie if you have too.

You're not leaving me.
Get the fuck out the cab.
You can't take the children,
you can't, I'm their dad.

Listen, you cunt.
I'm taking you to court,
not because I want the children,
but because I want it to hurt.

You lying slut,
you know it wasn't all my fault.
Do you think they'll believe you,
accusing me of assault?

Oh, you think you've won,
but I don't care what the judge said,
I'm going to kill you tonight,
you can't win if you're dead.

Once in Fort Carson

I smell the mixture,
of scents from the kitchen,
and the couch,
I hid beneath.

To the left of me,
is the hallway stretching miles,
it wasn't that long,
I'm mistaken.

And that's him chasing me,
down that never-ending hallway,
slamming shoulders into corners,
as I turn into the doorway,
to face a room with one exit,
blocked by the man,
who with a fist taught me,
you can't run from pain.

Because to the right,
is the simple wooden table,
in the dining room,
with bare walls
connected to the kitchen,
that smells so familiar to me,
but with a scent,
I can't place.

And there at that table,
sits my mom with sweaty hands,
looking out the glass door,
leading to the backyard,
which many a neighbor had visited,
always unaware,
that a few feet inside,
was a man reigning terror.

From the couch that I hid,
you can see the living room floor,
where my father lay,
on drunken nights.

Quinton A. Clawson

And in sobriety,
sat on that very couch,
watching sports,
with that smell from the kitchen.

And there I am again,
fleeing with my mother,
down that fucking long hallway,
my father at our heels,
just barely closing that door,
and bracing enough to flip the lock,
with windows nailed shut.

There we are,
cowered in the corner,
ready to die,
once in Fort Carson.

Welcome to Our Future

There's the theory that it begins with the child,
like the larva before the cocoon,
which emerges a moth,
and serves the greater purpose of continuing a species,
by the magnifying glass of those that have wings,
and God forbid you're a butterfly,
because that's wrong.

I've seen them wandering the halls of equal education,
equal since the day of gestation,
like were beyond any sense of difference,
using history as an inference,
to why that's a sin,
and we declare it a win,
by not acknowledging the truth.

So we say it is our way,
in this day,
when skin color is, "just a belief,"
That we pride ourselves in the determination,
that religion is just faith with a set of rules to determine our behavior,
but that shouldn't matter because we're equal,
and we know were full of shit.

We've taught them that independence matters,
while teaching them their opinion counts,
and in turn that has bred entitlement,
to which this author cannot acknowledge,
any child,
religion or color,
truly deserves,
without hard work,
pain,
criticism,
and a few bruises.

And I'm all for modernization,
but sometimes development can be a backwards trend,
like medieval knights defending a castle,
we choose to believe that equality is a universal truth to defend,
but it's not.

Quinton A. Clawson

We're not equal,
and that will sting to the many unfortunate souls born as I,
and the ones who take up arms in their honor,
like we really need it from someone who passes by,
the experience,
the emotion,
the only reasons we took up the cause in the first place.

I'm not saying that inequality,
is a product of saying:
he's black,
he's white,
he's yellow,
she's purple,
and I added her in just to avoid being sexist.
All I'm saying,
is our conviction for equality has led us to be unrealistic,
like the burgeoning teens we teach,
who know we're not speaking the truth,
but who have been so abused by our authority,
that we haven't taught them to think for themselves,
and who very rarely have the audacity to try something new,
like thinking in a different color.

We teach this while breeding moths,
who gasp at the thought of a butterfly,
because how can someone spread their wings if they're different?
How dare you tell me I'm not special,
when my mother told me I was,
and my father told me I was too,
and everything is so scary,
when nothing is new,
but that's what we breed.

We take the tests that evaluate the standards of our children,
the same ones who believe they're special,
while they're gray like everyone else.
Like the bird that sings the same song as its counterpart,
but can swear on the worms it craves,
it deserves a nest.
So we take them and we test them,
and God forbid he's bad at math,
because his painting will never add up to numbers.

Ruminating

We teach them that's all that counts,
but any mathematician will tell you,
its not about the numbers,
but about the amounts.
And if you can get to x,
by being a y,
and choosing to hang with z,
then what does it matter what pi is?

We're just moths,
who have been led to believe were butterflies,
through a cocoon of irrational lies,
that fill us with insecurity,
and when a butterfly comes along,
spreads it wings,
unique and strong,
we kill it.

Welcome to our future.

Quinton A. Clawson

My Foreboding Fraught

Through a pocket of serenity,
surrounded by chaos,
I see evidence of doom,
a slow decaying script,
like the clothes that begin to pile,
on the floor of a room.

And I'm quite aware,
how this act will end,
reserving my emotion,
like the curtains of a stage,
or the actor whose portraying death,
waiting for fin.

They send hellos my way,
I send them greetings back,
together they are friends,
alone they are just that,
and I pray it will be something more,
but I know how this play ends.

So I smile to feign normality,
and speak with lies between my teeth,
signing post cards that say,
goodbye, good luck, I believe in you,
but between the lines is reality,
and it's an opaque day.

For softened hearts have hardened,
meticulous minds made marks,
and it's all for naught,
swiftly swimming southward,
in an ingenious inkling ignorance,
farewell to you,
with my foreboding fraught.

Quinton A. Clawson

RELIGION

I have insulted many during discussions of religion.
It seems to me that religion has always been a coping mechanism, but never a necessity. It is a way of understanding the yet to be understood, and as such, has become a source of comfort to many.
I would never fathom to take meaning from an individual, but so long as we subject ourselves to unproven doctrines, we work against progress. With so much evidence to the contrary, I cannot comprehend how anyone could concede to the idea that we are helpless beings in need of an archaic creator, or that our fate is predetermined.
Humans have been, and will always be, so much more than what can be written down, and we hold more value than religion will ever give us credit for.

Quinton A. Clawson

He Stood Upon the Pulpit

He stood upon the pulpit,
in a glorious, brazen spectacle,
somewhere on Chapel Hill,
and as I remained skeptical.

He lifted his arms,
and in a flurry of speech,
damned us all to hell,
for as far as far could reach.

He spoke to the women,
who he blamed for our sin,
and he spoke to your children,
and he spoke to my kin.
And he spoke to the girls,
who he claimed were like whores,
and compared them to animals,
grazing on all fours.
He spoke to the boys,
for their insatiable lust,
until his face was burnt red,
like his blood were to bust.
And he spoke there to me,
because I'm a heathen too,
and when judgment day comes,
the day I will rue.

But it happened upon me,
as I sat there and listened,
that his robes were of silk,
and on his neck, gold glistened.

It just so happened,
that he spoke in rash wroth,
and every day he behaved,
like the sinning sullen sloth,
and it just so happened,
that he had been married a third time,
and so it seemed as he gleamed,
there was hypocrisy and crime.
It just so happened,

that his vanity wasn't hidden,
and a solemn sullen expression,
was with his wife's face ridden,
and it just so happened,
that as I sat there that day,
his pride and his ego,
had kept my belief at bay.

The Mirror

We are not who we see,
but what we believe we see,
like the sapling,
that is soon to be,
a tree.

You see, the key,
is that this tree,
was never given a mirror,
that told it to be,
what we see.

And it did not believe,
that it would not achieve,
what it would be,
because naturally,
is all it ever knew.

Yet ingeniously,
we envied thee,
so we structured a mirror,
that with,
defined me,
and what we believed,
to see.

And it is with hope,
that structurally,
metaphorically,
we hope to crumble,
that this belief,
of what we see,
is not you,
and is not me.

Quinton A. Clawson

Don't Tell Me It's Not Cereal

I have a bucket full of nails,
that I only eat at breakfast,
if God gave me a body,
then let me use it,
the way I feel fit.

Like living in a social standard worked for you,
or you,
or you…

Nail them to a plank,
and I'll tell you you're wrong,
cause subjective terms are great,
when you're not the subject,
of a constant scrutinizing gaze,
in an inadequate frame,
picking apart the perfect picture,
I use with every single purpose,
of a purported pretense,
that we were built with,
and your camera,
doesn't change the leaves of a tree,
or the independence,
of some lack luster sense,
that you're built in an image,
like opinions,
are suddenly law.

So I'll eat nails in the morning,
some screws at night,
with a book as a spoon,
and maybe morbidity instead of milk,
don't tell me it's not cereal.

Quinton A. Clawson

I Wondered Upon a Star

Does a star cry when it falls from the sky?
Or thank the universe for its time?
Does it bargain with its God?
Does it notice me?

I wished upon its death,
and gazed upon its sight.
I wonder if it heard me pray,
my desperate pleas that night.

I wonder if a star began,
when this star had ended,
and if that star has hopes and dreams,
and if its God had planned this.

It's a beautiful thought to think,
to grant wishes when you die,
and what other optimists,
made a wish that night?

I wonder what they wished for,
I wonder if it came true,
and I wonder if it's coincidence,
that the next day I met you.

Maybe it's silly to think,
that a star would take the time,
in the middle of its death,
to answer my cry.

But I don't think it's silly,
to admire the thought,
that if people were more like stars,
we'd be a beautiful lot.

Quinton A. Clawson

And Wouldn't You Know?

I believe,
in me,
and wouldn't you know?
Not much more.

Why beg for scraps,
when you have bread?
Why beg for words,
when enough is said?
Why talk to fantasies,
when alone with your mind,
and why believe in a ghost,
who justifies the killing,
of your own kind?

I believe,
in my thoughts,
and wouldn't you know?
They're not a warped subjective reality.

Like explanations are a necessity,
for misunderstood causes,
when nothing ever changes,
the unexpected losses.
Like logic isn't necessary,
when divinity doesn't make sense,
and that type of ignorance,
is why my thoughts,
are my lens.

I believe,
in my actions,
and wouldn't you know?
They don't have to be perfection.

Choices are not absurdity,
but a truth of our nature,
we're just animals reacting,
to our raw life's wager.
Every behavior has a reason,
and maybe not always justified,

but a dogma is just a perspective,
which for every reason,
should be tried.

I believe,
in humanity,
and wouldn't you know?
It doesn't need a savior.

Why beg for scraps,
when we can bake bread?
Why ask for words,
when we can write them instead?
Why talk to fantasies,
when together we could imagine,
and wouldn't you know,
if we did,
miracles could happen.

You Don't Matter

Do you really think a ghost in the sky,
cares if you live or die?
You really think what you do matters?

Do you really think there's the slightest chance,
that the truth is in the cant's,
like you can't talk in absolutes.

Do you really believe in omniscience,
and if so, that it'd have the patience,
the patience to deal with mistakes?

Tell me, you can't believe God is great,
while his followers pray and wait,
and if he hears you, he listens.

It'd be nice to believe in all of it,
that's why we choose ignorance,
but I promise,
you don't matter.

Quinton A. Clawson

POLITICS

Politics is nothing more than the variables relating to government. I take issue with politics, not because it exists, but because of the manner in which it exists. I believe in truth and evidence, and politics seems to be immune to these two conditions. Politics does not concern itself with what can be proven, but with raw emotion and personal perspective.
However, we must remember that politics does not exist without human involvement. Politics is not the monster, but the costume, and the true monsters, are those that choose to wear it.

Quinton A. Clawson

An Innocent Man's Execution

They strap me to a plastic bed,
and with a lever tilt my head,
to view those who have come as witness.

I find it just suspicious,
that it's not thought a sickness,
to want to watch any human die.

And from their seats they will cry,
it's my duty, and they'll lie,
a subconscious now free of burden.

But are they all certain,
there should be a curtain,
are they without doubt that I'm guilty?

And it seems a pity,
a girl oh so pretty,
now will never have her killer caught.

They give it little thought,
and find the perfect spot,
to partner their needle with my vein.

A little pain,
and I explain,
is this justice when a man is wrong?

With seconds long,
until I'm gone,
and you're the monster you think I am.

It gives a damn,
the soul of man,
what if I'm innocent when in death?

A last breath,
a flat breast,
an innocent man's execution.

Quinton A. Clawson

What Meets the Eye

I'd like to imagine,
that we are not so different,
but so different indeed,
that our differences,
refuse war,
and our indifferences,
trump greed.

I'd like to believe,
that you'll love me,
for my skin,
as well as my mind,
and I'll love your culture,
for as much,
as you love mine.

I'd like to dream,
in colors beyond the rainbow,
much more than imagined,
and that who you love,
is as beautiful,
as a heart less damaged.

My ideals are this,
we are the same,
but so different,
you and I,
but we're so much more,
than what meets the eye.

Quinton A. Clawson

What a Great Turnout

What a great turnout!
This congregation has certainly dismissed,
any concerns of the common man,
with arguments of semantics,
and a predisposition not to listen.

Great job everyone!
we can all go home now,
and leave further topics of discussion,
to the tangents of social media,
and the emotional recklessness,
of its users.

Let us not forget!
The paychecks in the mail,
which we were chosen to receive,
by those among the population,
who sought to prohibit greed.

Let us celebrate!
The dismissal of our morals,
and the ethics of our oaths.
The misguided beliefs,
of those who were self-blinded,
and followed us in droves.

Let us cheer!
The dribbling of mass media,
and their superficial focus,
the ineptitude of journalism,
and the bias of the news.

Let's organize a parade!
Ran by two elite parties,
and let's choose a consulate,
to further the separation,
between the jackasses,
and those who don't forget.

Let us revel!
In the debauchery of propaganda,
with the intent of winning,
at any cost,
and let's call it, "the greater good".

Let us vote!
Refusal shall be unpatriotic,
leaving the constitution in tatters,
and we'll call his choice electoral,
yours shall be popular,
and when it all boils down,
none of this matters.

White Castle

In blackened citadels of armor,
screamed the vultures.
Upon the towers,
swore the rage of man.
Upon the fields,
begged the farmers.

In the King's castle,
voted by fools,
in a white dress,
masking truth.
He crumbled the ignorance,
that had voted for him.

The lords of the citadels,
were too busy squabbling,
the peasants too easily distracted,
by the town square jokers,
while the scholars,
were hung by their necks.

The books were burned,
in "righteous" pyres,
fueled by the emotions
of a convicted generation,
who's beliefs brainwashed,
the empire's youth.

And on the eve of conquer,
we cheered the charge,
applauded the man,
applauded the men,
who took everything from us,
with our permission.

Quinton A. Clawson

Black Lives Matter

How does someone tell,
those he doesn't know,
that he's sorry,
for the acts of a stranger?

Perhaps in a whisper,
a solemn gesture?
Perhaps with a fist,
a fury of violent justice?

How does one express,
the undeniable fact,
that innocent lives are lost,
and will never come back?

I think it starts,
with the simple acceptance,
that there's a problem,
and we need to address it.

I think it begins with empathy,
because we're all human,
and without each other,
we welcome our ruin.

I think it continues,
with perseverance to resistance,
and an idea that it will get better,
if we offer our assistance.

I think the catalyst is a voice,
that raises above the hate,
because life is not an issue,
that sanity debates.

Black lives matter,
and I'm sorry my friends,
that we as a people,
have failed you again.

Quinton A. Clawson

So Little Left to Say

I have so little left to say,
to the American,
who thinks this is somehow justified.

That patriotism,
is a warped sense of nationalism,
and that words don't matter,
when they're used haphazardly,
in every situation,
that there is an explanation,
for the lies,
and the deceit,
and every moment that the country,
has suffered the experience,
of a leader's tantrum,
in an unprofessional display.

I have so little patience left,
for so many to ignore reality,
and to determine,
that with which they disagree,
is fake,
like the truth isn't absolute,
and somehow,
an alternative is logical,
when there is no alternative,
to action.

I am so weary,
of every dismissal,
and every blind eye,
like only seeing is believing.
The focus is shifted,
and so we ignore the existence,
of an issue we created,
like the sick man,
who swears he'll get better,
if he just waits.

Quinton A. Clawson

I am so very tired,
like insomnia became politics,
and with the restlessness,
comes frustration,
because it's all so obvious,
but yet so unaccepted,
like the answer is on the shelf,
but we're reaching for the counter,
with insatiable responses,
that leave me starving.

I am finished.
The dribbling of incessant claims,
is far past completion.
The ineptitude of the mind,
is past resilience.
How would you expect,
with turned heads,
for dogs not to bite,
when they whine for chow,
but you only offer beatings?

SHORT STORIES

I've always enjoyed writing short stories. They offer fulfillment for those of us who struggle to finish a full-length novel, and they are brief enough to avoid boring a public that has a limited attention span.

I also enjoy writing short stories because they efficiently make powerful statements. Most of my statements are made with loose ends, so if you are enraged by the lack of a happy ending, continue no further.

Quinton A. Clawson

Leave a Light On

A man staggered into his small suburban house around midnight. The only light left on was the one from the kitchen, and as the man tried to creep silently to the stairs, karma, or maybe it was the alcohol, had a different plan. His foot met the leg of the living room couch, and a loud crash echoed across the room as he stumbled and caught himself on the back cushions.

"Shit," he whispered.

The man held his breath a moment, scanning the stairs leading to the second floor for a sign of life, and his fear was realized. The stairway light flickered on.

"Brian?"

Brian's wife tiptoed down the steps, her long pink robe grazing the carpeted floor. She stopped in the middle of the stairs and gazed at her husband with wide eyes.

"What are you doing? Are you just getting home?"

Brian did his best not to look guilty.

"Yea, sorry sweetie."

He swallowed the lump in his throat and turned for the kitchen, a subconscious avoidant behavior. His wife followed him as he entered the room with the linoleum floors. Brian turned on the Keurig, one of the few niceties they had.

"Well?" he heard his wife say.

Brian grabbed a mug from an overhead cabinet, placed a k-cup in the Keurig's open slot, and began brewing. He turned to face his wife, she was cross-armed and staring.

"Well what?"

"Are you kidding me?"

Brian's mind scrambled.

"I got stuck at work."

"Doing what?"

"Working."

"Don't lie to me."

"I'm not. What's with the interrogation?"

"I'm not stupid Brian. I know you weren't working, I can smell the alcohol on your breath."

Brian sighed as he looked at the floor and then back up at his wife. He leaned against the kitchen counter.

"Alright, I had a few beers with the guys, is that a crime?"

"It is when you're lying to me about it!"

There was silence, the hissing from the Keurig stopped, and Brian grabbed for the mug of coffee.

"It's her isn't it?"

Brian froze. He turned again to face his wife.

"What are you going on about?"

"I'm not naive Brian. I know you've been seeing that woman from work."

"What woman?"

"Don't play dumb!"

"Mom?"

The voice came from behind them. In the doorway was their young son, only six now. He gazed up at them with innocent eyes. In his hands he clutched a blanket that he had brought from his bed. His mother kneeled down lovingly.

"Timothy, what are you doing up sweetie?"

"I heard a noise."

"Timothy go back upstairs and go to bed, everything's fine, mommy and daddy are just talking."

Brian put the mug to his lips and took a sip of the coffee. Timothy gazed up at the stern hard face of his father and then turned to leave. His mother spun around and glared.

"Are you happy now? You woke Timothy."

"I woke him? I did? What about you with all of your yelling?"

"Keep your voice down!"

"It's a little late for that, isn't it?"

"Tell me the truth Brian."

"I am."

"Stop lying."

"All right, fine, you want the truth?"

Brian stopped leaning on the counter and took a stoic stance, like a soldier at attention. His wife's eyes widened. He took a close look at her face. He remembered a time when he had loved her, when that face was the very reason he got out of bed every morning, but somehow, that time had gone. She was worn now, he was worn, and it seemed that all the love they had once shared had traveled to a distant place.

"I'm unhappy. Is that better? I hate this, I hate us, and I hate this place."

"So what then? Cheating on me is how you plan on fixing that?"

"I never said that."

"Then what are you saying?"

Tears began to well up in Laurie's eyes. Brian knew it wasn't her fault, and that this was more than just a failed marriage. He could try to explain it to her, but it was much easier to get angry. It was much easier to throw insults at his family until the bonds that tied them had broken into such disrepair that he could finally escape, so that's what he did.

"I'm saying if it wasn't for Timothy, I wouldn't still be here."

His wife gasped, and then silence fell on them as they both realized that they were at a loss for words. Brian had said everything that needed to be said, and his wife had held on for as long as she possibly could.

Their voices didn't have to travel far to be heard in that small worn house. On the steps by the bannister, the little boy listened, fully aware now that it was his fault that his parents were so miserable.

"I'm leaving," said Brian.

His wife didn't answer. Brian set the mug of coffee on the counter, and then strode past her into the living room towards the door. As he passed by the couch that was the cause for all of this, he looked up at the bannister where his son peered down at him through lonely eyes. Brian stopped for a moment, trying to think of something to say, and then chose to allow silence to be his answer. He continued to the door, opened it, and then stepped over the perimeter of resentment that had slowly built around them. As he turned to close the door behind him, he noticed the figure of his wife silhouetted by the kitchen light, staring in his direction.

"Leave a light on," he said.

The door slammed shut, and from the other side of that broken house came his wife's reply.

"No, not anymore."

Quinton A. Clawson

Until Death Do Us Part

"He hits me mom."

The lights were dim in the suburban home. The two ladies sat at the kitchen table, speaking in hushed voices to avoid waking the man sleeping upstairs.

"Mom did you hear me?"

"Yes I heard you, keep it down or you'll wake your father."

Mrs. Williams stared at the family photo on the china cabinet that pressed against the wall, opposite from where she sat. Her, her husband, and her daughter had posed beautifully for the camera that New Year's Day a few years ago. It was in essence, the spitting image of the perfect family.

Her daughter sat quietly for a moment, tears running down her face. Her puffy red cheeks did nothing to compliment her long, sleek brown hair. Above her left eye, the skin beneath the eyebrow had begun to bruise and swell. As she gasped and choked to keep her sobbing silent, Mrs. Williams realized that the woman sitting here tonight was nowhere near the woman that she remembered in the photo.

"I warned you about that man," said Mrs. Williams.

Her daughter didn't meet her eyes, but answered solemnly below a hung head.

"I know."

"And now you've made your bed, so you will sleep in it."

This time her daughter's face rose to meet that of Mrs. Williams. Her pupils widened in shock and horror.

"You can't be serious mom. He's hitting me."

"I am. You are married now. You will find a way to fix this."

"But mom…"

"No. You will go home to him tonight, and you will think about how you can be a better wife in the future."

"A better wife? What are you saying? That this is my fault?"

Mother and daughter stared at each other. Mrs. Williams held a scornful look upon her face as her daughter's lips trembled with fear.

"I'm saying that we are people of God. I'm not sure what you thought it meant when you said until death do us part, but it did not mean you could run out on him. A good wife does not fall back on her vows just because of a few disagreements."

There was silence as the daughter held her mother's glare.

"Disagreements."

"Yes," said Mrs. Williams.

More silence as the night seemed to impact upon them. Through more tears and pleading, Mrs. Williams stood her ground. She refused to offer her daughter a haven, because although she disapproved of her daughter's choice in love, her daughter was married now, and vows had been made. The daughter's husband would come collect his wife, and the daughter would go home with her husband without another word to her mother.

Tomorrow, Mrs. Williams would wake up, and she would sit down to watch the morning news like she always did. There would be a knock at the door, but she would ignore for the breaking news that had just been mentioned on the television.

"Honey, what's wrong?" Mr. Williams would ask as he entered from the kitchen.

There would be another knock at the door, and Mrs. Williams would answer her husband with some sobbing. The mention of a murder and a suicide would repeat itself from the television.

It hadn't been what Mrs. Williams had hoped for, but it was until death do us part.

Through the Window

There she was, on top of her secret lover, unknowingly mocking me from the other side of the window. Her back arched as she straddled him. As she closed her eyes and gasped in pleasure, her perky breasts jumped to let me know that this wasn't a dream.

From where I knelt outside her bedroom window, I could see the picture frame on her nightstand. It had been placed face down, hiding the photo of us. Beside it, I could see the engagement ring I had given her, during a candlelit dinner, shimmer in the moonlight.

She placed her hands on her hips and rotated around him like water circling the drain. He reached up and grabbed a hold of her shoulders. His strong, muscular, hairy arms wrapped around her, and he tossed her below him so that he could show his dominance, so that he could dominate everything that I had ever loved.

He thrusted against her in my direction, unknowingly destroying the gates of the castle I had built in that very place. For a moment, he gazed upward, through the window that I too peered through. Above the headboard of the bed, he met my eyes. They widened as he realized that this hadn't been a private matter. Did he know that I had just called her? Did he know that lying on the ground before me were the flowers that I had brought in surprise? Did he even know I existed?

In an instant he detached himself from where he perched between her legs. I could hear their voices ring out through the window.

"He's outside!"

"Who?" she asked.

"Your fiancé."

So it was then that I knew this wasn't a mistake. I dipped below the window, and turned so that my back rested against the wall. I pulled my knees to my chest, and wrapped my arms around them in comfort. I rocked steadily back and forth, no longer holding the tears that were suppressed by astonishment. Their voices continued behind me, muffled by the brick that was once a solid foundation.

A better man may have burned with anger. A better man may have marched to the front door and demanded entrance. A better man may have unleashed the rage of betrayal upon his fiancé's lover, but then again, I was not a better man. I was a man who knew when a war was not worth fighting, and instead, took refuge in succumbing to the wounds of the heart.

Through the tears that I shared with my fiancé's exterior wall, I knew it was all over. I knew I could no longer kid myself about the fairy tale romance that I thought we shared. I knew that in a few months, a few years, maybe I would consider it for the best, but then, in that moment, I wished I hadn't looked through the window.

Quinton A. Clawson

That Taxi Ride

"You alright Vick?"

Henry's voice shakes me from my trance. I realize I've been staring at the liquor bottles behind the bar for far too long.

"Yea I'm fine."

"Don't look like it."

I shift in my stool.

"It's nothing man, just this fucking call I had last night."

Henry laughs. He picks up a rocks glass filled with whiskey on ice, and puts it to his lips. He takes a meaningful sip, and then sets the glass back down.

"So what happened?"

I lean forward, rest my elbows on the bar, and wrap my hands around the chill of the beer bottle in front of me. I look up at the TV in the center of the wall above the beer taps, but I'm not watching whatever's on. I'm thinking, and what I think is that maybe Henry might understand what's been bothering me. I think, being a taxi driver like me, he might get it. So I decide to tell him.

"So I picked up this couple last night."

"Yea?"

"Yea, a good looking middle-aged couple down in the business district."

"Ok."

"So the guy waves me down, I pull over, and they begin climbing in. As they climb in, the guy tells me they're going to Antonio's, you know, that fancy Italian place downtown."

"Oh yea, my brother's been there, says it's a nice joint."

I glance at Henry. He's not a bad guy, but the last thing you would say about him is that he's upscale. I wonder for a moment what his brother is like, and if he's anything like Henry, how he managed to make his way into a place like Antonio's. I decide not to push the subject.

"Anyway," I say. "They settle in, and I start driving. So I'm looking at them through my rearview mirror, making small talk like I do for the customers who actually care to have a conversation. They're nice, you know? They're holding hands, and the guys bragging about the night he has planned for them. The lady, well she's just staring up at him as he talks as if he's the only thing she cares about in this world."

"So what's the problem?"

"I'm getting there."

I lift the bottle in my hands and take a swig. Henry pulls a cigarette from the pack he keeps in his jean jacket pocket, places the cigarette between his lips, and lights it up. Smoke billows around the two of us.

"So the more he talks, the more this guy seems familiar, and I start getting the feeling that I know him from somewhere. So he keeps talking, and I keep squinting at him through the rearview mirror trying to figure it out, while this lady is just gazing up at him like he's God."

"So did you know the guy?"

"Yea, we were a few blocks away from Antonio's when it finally hit me, he's one of my regulars."

"So what's the problem?"

"The problem is, he's never with the same girl."

"Oh man, so she was a hooker?"

"No, not this one."

Henry takes a sip of his whiskey, sets the rocks glass back down on the bar, and then turns to me suddenly with wide eyes.

"Oh shit man, his wife?"

"Now you got it."

"How could you tell?"

"The ring on her finger, and the way she was looking at him, no hooker looks at a guy that way."

"Wow that's fucked up."

Henry takes a puff of his cigarette and another sip of his whiskey.

"So then what happened?"

"So I realize this, right? This is the same guy that I pick up from the business district some nights, scantily dressed woman on his arm, and take to a motel somewhere nearby. Same guy that calls me later to have me pick him up. I don't care, right? I mean, it's not my business what this guy does in his spare time."

"Do you think he recognized you?"

"That's the thing, I think he knew who I was from the moment he stepped into my cab."

"What makes you say that?"

"Well, we get to Antonio's, and he passes me some money as I call out his fare. I can't remember how much he owed me, but it wasn't much."

"Yea, downtown's not a long drive from the business district."

"Exactly, but when I look at the money in my hand, I realize he's handed me a hundred. I look in the rearview mirror, we make eye contact, and he says, 'keep it'."

"Damn, so what's the problem? I'd be fucking overjoyed."

"I was, for that split instant, and then everything changed."

"What? Did he take the money back?"

Henry lets out a laugh and picks up his whiskey. He shakes around the ice, and it jingles inside the glass. He takes a sip to finish it, puts the glass back down, and then takes a long drag of his cigarette before he puts that out in the ashtray in front of him.

"No, nothing like that."
"Then what?"
I take a sip of my beer.
"He winked at me."
Henry starts laughing again.
"He winked at you?"
"Yea."
"So?"
"Are you kidding me Henry?"
"I don't see the big deal man."

Henry lights up another cigarette, and I take a sip of my beer. I see the bartender point silently to Henry's empty glass, and Henry nods to signal that he wants another.

"Listen, he winked at me like I was in on it, like I was an accomplice at his shitty game of being an asshole."

"I don't want to be a dick man, but you kind of are."

I finish my beer, and set the empty bottle down on the bar. The bartender arrives with Henry's fresh drink, and gives me the same nonverbal signal to ask if I want another. I nod.

"Look man," says Henry. "It's like you said before, what do you care what this guy does in his free time?"

I want to think Henry's right. I want to tell myself that it's none of my business. I want to believe that I can remain neutral and impartial to the shitty customers that come with the job.

"You should've seen her face Henry."
"Whose?"
"The wife's."
Henry picks up his whiskey and takes a sip.
"It's not your problem man."

For Henry, that's it, that's all that needs to be said. I envy him. I wish I could go back to the way it was before that taxi ride, but the same two images keep replaying inside my head. The wife smiles adoringly at her husband, and her husband winks at me through the rearview mirror.

The bartender brings me another beer, and I take a long swig. Henry puffs his cigarette, and he drinks more whiskey. He laughs to himself as he gazes at the TV behind the bar.

"Man, the Yankees have a shit pitcher this year."

I don't answer. I'm picturing something worse than heartbreak, years of ignorance. I'm picturing the wife smiling at her husband every time he gets home, every time she cooks him dinner, and every time they make love. Something's changing in me, I can feel it. I can feel it as clearly as I hear Henry speak.

"You alright Vick?"

Quinton A. Clawson

The Bee

So there's this bee... I know that's an odd way to begin a story, but just listen. There's this bee, and it lands on the cushions of a loveseat in front of me. I'm sitting out back, having a beer, and I watch it.

It lands on the cushions of the loveseat, and for whatever reason, it just starts laying into it with its stinger. I'm not a bee, so I can't say what its motivation was, but I imagine it felt threatened. Now that may seem odd to you, but you're probably not a bee either, so don't judge.

Now this isn't a wasp or a hornet, but a bee, so I already know what fate has in mind for this tiny creature. I lean back in my chair and pull out a cigar; not one of the fancy ones, but one of those small stick cigars you find at the gas station. I light it up, and I wait. I watch as the bee kicks its tiny legs about, struggling either to inflict pain or dislodge its stinger. The thing shakes and trembles and twists, and it quickly becomes a pathetic sight.

As the bee's movements slow, I know it's time is coming to an end. I take a swig of my beer, and a puff of my cigar. I start to wonder about this bug, much more than I think I've ever wondered about an insect. Its whole life had led up to this point, and I'm not an entomologist, so I can't tell you how long that life was, but it certainly seemed a waste.

Not much changes, and I grow bored. I pull out my phone and open the YouTube app to some video about the top ten funniest cat videos or something, I can't really remember to tell you the truth. I watch, and I laugh, but every so often I peer over the edge of my phone to look at the bee. Every time I do, it's still in the same spot it was before, maybe having shifted an inch one way or the next. I watch video after video, all the meanwhile keeping tabs on the bee, which eventually rests in an awkward hugging position on the cushion.

I take a picture of it. I don't know why, but I do. I stare at it for a long time while its lifeless body just sits there with its stinger stuck in the cushion, and I feel a sadness creeping up on me. I know the feeling, it's the same feeling one gets when they're saying goodbye to a loved one. It's the same feeling I felt when my dog died, and maybe it wasn't as strong as I had felt it before, but it was there.

I decide to move from my chair to the empty cushion on the loveseat, next to the bee. I glance at it, and put my arm around the back of the cushion like I'm hanging out with a good friend. I open up the YouTube app on my phone again. I watch another stupid video about something stupid that will never amount to anything but something stupid. I start getting angry.

I move back to my chair and quietly glare at the bee's dead body. Why did it have to die? Why did it have to be so stupid? I begin to realize I might be crazy.

I wonder if it had a family, and I realize that a bee doesn't care for such things. Or does it? Maybe it does, and maybe it doesn't, but that doesn't make a difference because it's what I think about. I wonder if bees believe in burials.

I stand up and go inside to grab a beer. I decide that I'm not going to put so much thought into a creature that's life amounted to stinging a cushion to death because that is insignificant to the greater scheme of things. I realize that I've spent my entire night watching videos on YouTube, and I realize that I'm insignificant to the greater scheme of things.

I go back outside, and I light up another cigar. I watch the bee closely, waiting for any movement that would imply it's still alive. It doesn't move, and I feel the weight of the world crash down on me. Why did it have to die?

I convince myself that I need to bury it, only because if I left it on the cushion that would be gross, but I know I have ulterior motives. I poke it with my finger, and it doesn't move. I put one open palm on the edge of the cushion while I use my other hand to brush it into my grasp. The bee doesn't struggle any more.

I carry its lifeless body to a small patch of ground next to the concrete slab that sits in my backyard. I wonder again if bees believe in burials, and I realize it doesn't matter. I use my hand like a trowel and dig a small hole, and for some reason I don't care that dirt is getting inside my fingernails. I lay the bee gently in the hole.

I watch it a moment, and I say a small prayer. I'm not religious. I wonder if bees are, but again it doesn't matter. Nothing matters, and the issue of politics, religion, and economics seems silly. I cover the hole with dirt.

I take a rock and I place it over the mound of dirt that now sits as a burial tomb for the bee. I return to my chair and take a swig of my beer. I decide to light another cigar. I take my phone out of my pocket, but instead of opening the YouTube app, I take a look at the picture of the bee. I think I miss him, or her, I'm not really sure how to tell the gender of a bee. I'm definitely crazy.

I put my phone away. I take another swig of my beer, and I take another puff of my cigar. The stars in the sky seem to dim. I think the world is getting heavier, but I'm too drunk to tell. I look over at the burial site of the bee. I hope his family doesn't miss him, or her, it doesn't matter. I feel a tear escape my eye, but that's stupid because it's for a bee. I'm a bee though, at least, as significant as one. I wonder if someone would take the time to scoop my body from a cushion… probably not.

NOTHING REALLY ENDS

Nothing really ends my friend. Sure, you'll reach the last page of a book, the last bite of a meal, and the last breath of your life, but time, existence, or whatever you want to call it, marches on.

www.ingramcontent.com/pod-product-compliance
Lightning Source LLC
Chambersburg PA
CBHW061329040426
42444CB00011B/2839